CRAZY CHRISTIANS

Andy Robb

Copyright © John Hunt Publishing Ltd
46A West Street, Alresford, Hants SO24 9AU, UK
Tel: +44 (0) 1962 736880 Fax: +44 (0) 1962 736881
E-mail: office@johnhunt-publishing.com
www.johnhunt-publishing.com

Text © 2003 Andy Robb
Illustrations © 2003 Andy Robb
Design by Nautilus Design, UK
Page layout by Andy Robb

ISBN 1 84298 122 6

Scriptures quoted from the Good News Bible published by The Bible
Societies/HarperCollins Publishers Ltd., UK

A CIP catalogue record for this book is available from the British Library.

Printed in Singapore by TWP

CONTENTS

Introduction	5
A Whirlwind Tour of the Bible	9
Why God Made the World in the First Place	13
The Christmas Story	28
In the Tabernacle	30
A Raw Deal for Animals	32
Some Famous Christians	39
Christianity – Special Offer	58
Top Ten List of Things that Spoil the World	67
Top Ten List of Things that Make the World Better	68
Action Stations	75
The Great Resurrection Riddle	89
God's Promises	119
The Christian Calendar	122
Bitesize Bible Bitz	124

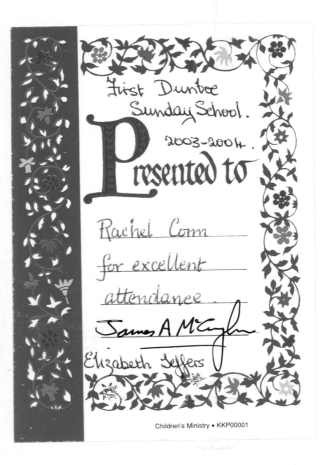

First Dundee
Sunday School.
2003-2004.

Presented to

Rachel Corm

for excellent

attendance

James A M°Caughan

Elizabeth Jeffers

Children's Ministry • KKP00001

Interesting-ish Intro

If you've ever got round to reading any of the other Boring Bible books
(and if you haven't then I hope you've got a very good reason!)
then there's one thing you'll probably have discovered and it's this ...

THE BIBLE IS ANYTHING BUT BORING!

(To be perfectly honest, if you've been paying attention then you should have discovered a good few more things than just that but don't worry, I'm not going to test you.)

In fact, as far many people are concerned the Bible is absolutely, **100%** the most exciting book they've ever clapped eyes on.

THIS IS ABSOLUTELY, 100% THE MOST EXCITING BOOK I'VE EVER CLAPPED EYES ON!

Quite!
The point I was about to make before I was rather rudely interrupted was that it's no good just *reading* the Bible like a story book (however interesting you may find it), unless you actually *do* something with it.

Let me give you an example.
Supposing someone gives you a recipe book ...

Er, thanks.
And then all you ever do is just read it without ever having a go at any of the tasty suggestions. It's not going to be much use, now, is it?

See what I mean?

It's the same with the Bible (but without the ingredients bit).
God didn't just give it to us so we'd have something to flick
through when we've got five minutes to spare.
The Bible is God's very own **supa-dupa** recipe book
and it's crammed full of loads and loads of juicy things to get
your teeth stuck into.

And if you don't believe me then here's a little taster of some of
the stuff you're going to find out as you read on.

1.How to become a saint
(*without* being dead for three
hundred years).

2.Why a piece of fruit isn't
always *quite* as good for you
as your mum and dad would
have you believe!

3.Where your top secret
codename is kept. (And I'll bet
you didn't even know you *had*
one, did you?)

4.Why God's got millions of
homes (and where they are).

The thing is, if you don't put into action what you've actually
read in the Bible then it's a complete **waste of your time**.
Anyway, on with the book.

First Things First

Now, one of the main things you're going to find out in this book is what exactly a Christian is (that's if you don't know already) and how you can become one (that's if you want to). (If you want to find out *why* this book's called '**Crazy** Christians' you'll need to stick with me.)

Fascinating Fact:

Some Christians are called 'born again' Christians but according to the Bible all Christians are 'born again' Christians, because every Christian has to be 'born again'. All it means is getting a new start in life – but more of that later.

The problem we've got is that if we dive right into the bit about Christians straight off without telling you *why* it's a really good idea to become one then you'll miss out on some of the best bits.

So I figure it would be in everyone's best interests if first of all we shoot off on a whirlwind tour of the history of the world (as taken from the Bible) and check out what's been going on that we should know about.

Are you with me?...

Good!
Then what are we waiting for?
Let's get *going*.

A WHIRLWIND TOUR OF THE BIBLE

Go! Go! Go!

The first thing that's been going on is ... God making the world.
Some people think that the world came about by chance – as a
result of a whopping great cosmic explosion.
A **big bang**, in fact.

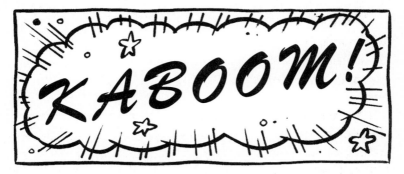

But that would mean that you're nothing more than a bit of an
accident which doesn't sound right to me.
So here's what I want you to do.
Find yourself a mirror ...
(Do not, I repeat, **do not** use a car wing mirror, especially if it's
on a moving car – let's be a bit sensible out this!)
Okay, now take a look at your reflection.
Hey, not bad, eh?
Look a bit closer.
You eyes are fascinating, aren't they?

Did you know ... that your eyes are made up of **137 million** special cells?

As light enters your eyes through the lens it is changed into electric signals which travel along your optic nerve to your brain at an almost supersonic **300 miles an hour**! Your brain uses millions of electrical connections to turn the signals into pictures, just like a TV camera works only *much better*!

Okay, you can stop admiring yourself in the mirror. I want you to hold out your hands, palms up.

Now look at your hands ...

Now look at your hands ...
please.

Did you know ... that there's nobody on this earth with the same fingerprints as you?

The squiggly design on your fingertips is *totally unique.* They're a one-off.

That's why the police often use fingerprints to track down criminals – because they each match only *one* person.

And last but not least I want you to bend down and touch your toes (or as near as you can get to them without doing yourself an injury).

Did you know ... that without a skeleton inside you you'd be nothing more than a wobbly, jelly-like lump, flopping all over the place?

In fact you wouldn't even be able to stand up to start with.
Your skeleton is **brilliant**!
Not only does it stop you wobbling all over the place like
something out of 'Flubber' but it's
got loads of joints that mean you
can bend over and do things like
touching your toes.

The joints have even got a cushion
of gristle round them to stop them
rubbing and they're lubricated by
special liquids, just like oil
lubricates the parts of a machine.
(Oops! I forgot to tell you to straighten up. Let's hope you're not
still touching your toes).

All in all, you are **amazing**!
And the Bible says that the reason you're so amazing is that you
were made by **God**.

The Bible also says that thousands of years ago God made the
world's very *first* people and while he was at it he made
everything else as well.

Stars, planets, trees, flowers and animals
... **the whole lot**!
(Boring Bible book *Ballistic Beginnings* has
got loads more stuff about this bit of the
Bible).
You name it, God made it.

(No, not things like TV's and computers
– you're just being silly. You know exactly what I mean).

That's a good question.
To find out the answer you're going to need to use your imagination, so switch it on ...

... and keep reading.

Chomp! Chomp! Chomp!

The Bible tells us that God is love.
It doesn't say he *sometimes* loves or even that he's very loving but that he *is* love.
That means he needs something to love or it's all gonna go to waste.

That's where *we* come in ...

God made people just so he could have someone to love.

And to top it off he made the world especially for us to live in.

The downside to that was that God's very first people Adam and Eve (you've probably heard of them) rejected his love by disobeying him.

The world's first couple were given the run of planet earth and allowed to eat absolutely anything they wanted with one gi-normous exception.

(That's not including animals – *they* didn't get on to the menu until later in history).

The Tree of the Knowledge of Good and Evil was strictly **out of bounds**!

A munch of the fruit of *that* tree would have meant the end to Adam and Eve's innocence and purity.

But munch it they did.

And that, sad to say, was the end of people's friendship with God.

(Well for a while at least, but you'll have to read on if you want to discover the *full* facts.)

Glug! Glug! Glug!

According to the Bible things went downhill from then on.
God was left with no choice but to wipe all the wicked people
off the face of the earth before they completely *ruined* his
creation.

God sent the world's worst flood
to cover the face of the earth so
that even the mountain peaks
were under water.

Fortunately for us there was at
least *one* good guy around.

He went by the name of Noah
and God instructed him to build a
boat to keep him and his family
safe (not forgetting two of every
kind of animal) so that the earth
could be repopulated once the
flood waters had subsided.

Fascinating Fact:

*If you check out the book of Genesis in the Bible
and head for chapter 5 you can calculate exactly
how many years it was from the beginning of time
until God's flood hit the earth.*

If you don't own a Bible then have a go at working it out by
adding up the ages of the world's first people listed here ...

Adam was 130 when he had his son Seth.
Seth was 105 when he had his son Enosh.
Enosh was 90 when he had his son Kenan.
Kenan was 70 when he had his son
Mahalalel (trying saying *that* quickly).
Mahalalel was 65 when he had his son
Jared.
Jared was 162 when he had his son Enoch.
Enoch was 65 when he had his son
Methuselah (the world's oldest man).
Methuselah was 187 when he had his son Lamech.
Lamech was 182 when he had his son Noah.
Noah was 600 when God sent the flood.

I make it **1,656** years in total from the beginning of time up
until the flood. Do you agree?

Bam! Bam! Bam!

Sure enough, thanks to Noah and his fellow passengers on the
ark (an ark is what the Bible calls Noah's boat) the world soon
began to fill up with people and animals again.
The plants started to sprout and fruit began to appear on the
trees. Everything in the garden was looking rosy ...

Unfortunately, things didn't stay that way for long ...

It seemed that something had got into people when they'd turned their backs on God at the very beginning of the world, and however hard they tried, they just couldn't seem to stop being bad.

This wasn't much of a surprise to God and he already had an idea up his sleeve.

Meet Abram ...

Abram had been handpicked by God to start a brand new nation of people who would do their level best to love God and to obey him.

First off, Abram (later called Abraham, just to confuse you) had to leave his nice home and head for the plot of land where this new nation was going to live.

It was called Canaan if you're really interested and it was right here ...

Being on the move meant living in a **tent** from now on ...

After more than his fair share of adventures (check out Boring Bible book *Hotchpotch Hebrews* for more info) Abram was succeeded by his son Isaac who *also* had to put up with living in a tent.

Not to be outdone by his dad, Jacob (Isaac's son) *also* continued the family tradition of camping.

Boring Bible Fact:
This new nation, that began with Abram, were called the Israelites (although they were also known as the Hebrews or *even* the Jews).

Grow! Grow! Grow

Before the Israelites had even *thought* about starting to build cities and towns they were up and off out of Canaan (for 430 years to be precise) to live in Egypt.

Boring Bible Joke:
Why didn't the Israelite women who had children mind going to Egypt? Because it was a good place for mummies!

The move to Egypt was all thanks
to a guy called Joseph ...

... and a particularly nasty famine.

The upside of relocating to sunny Egypt was they got to live in
houses.

The Israelites might have temporarily moved out of Canaan, but
God was still very much with them.
The Bible says that they continued to grow in number which
really scared the Egyptians.

Why was that, you may ask?

I said, "*May* ask".
I didn't say you *had* to ask!
Anyway, before I tell you the answer there's one small thing I forgot to mention.
The Israelites, having been invited to weather the famine in Egypt, had in the meantime ended up becoming the Egyptians' slaves.
(A bit of raw deal if you ask me).

Egypt had a new Pharoah (or king) who wasn't half as sympathetic to the Israelites as the previous one had been.
The bigger their number, the greater the threat the Israelites became if they suddenly decided to rebel against their masters.

So Pharaoh decided to make life hard for them –
but luckily for the Israelites, God was having none of it.

I HAVE SEEN HOW CRUELLY MY PEOPLE
ARE BEING TREATED IN EGYPT.
I HAVE HEARD THEM CRY OUT TO BE
RESCUED FROM THEIR SLAVE
DRIVERS. I KNOW ALL ABOUT YOUR
SUFFERINGS AND SO I HAVE COME
DOWN TO RESCUE YOU FROM THE
EGYPTIANS AND BRING YOU OUT OF
EGYPT TO A SPACIOUS LAND.

He sent in his special hit-man, Moses (of bullrushes fame) to set
them free and get them back to Canaan.
With the help of a some *awful* plagues the Pharaoh was
persuaded to let the Israelites go.
With the help of some *awesome* miracles (you can read up about
them in Boring Bible book *Magnificent Moses*) God got them out
of there.

Plod! Plod! Plod!

You'd think that, all things considered, the Israelites would have
been extremely grateful to God for what he'd
done.

SURE
WOULD!

Nothing of the sort!
No sooner were the Israelites on their way
than they started to grumble and moan about
anything and everything.

They made Moses' life a misery.

All in all they'd have preferred to return to Egypt as slaves rather than have to rough it for a few weeks until they got to Canaan.

God had had it with their moaning.

As a punishment, none of the grumblers ever made it to Canaan.

The Israelites had to wander around in the desert for forty years until they'd all died out.

Biff! Biff! Biff!

At long last, with all the moaners and groaners dead and buried, the Israelites entered Canaan.

Well, it wasn't *quite* as simple as that.

There was just the small matter of the people who were already living there to be sorted.

Moses was now dead and the Israelites' new leader, Joshua, had a few tricky decisions to make.

Should he just politely ask the present inhabitants to leave?

Or perhaps ...

Or even ...

Which is just what the Israelites did.
The inhabitants of Canaan were a particularly wicked bunch and Bible says that God gave orders for them all to be destroyed. If they weren't destroyed then the Israelites wouldn't have anywhere to live, so they didn't really have much choice, did they?

(They could have stayed in the desert, I suppose, but that probably didn't sound much of an option.)

ADVANCE WARNING:
THIS NEXT SECTION IS A REAL
WHOPPER SO BRACE YOURSELF!

Up! Down! Up! Down! Up Down!

For your information, the Israelites never *quite* got round
to getting rid of all the inhabitants of Canaan, but they
did manage to take control of *most* of the land.
At long last God's special nation started to settle down.
They built towns and they built cities ...

In fact, they even changed the name of the place and
called it ...

With a permanent land of their own the Israelites were meant to be a good example to the surrounding nations of how God wanted people to live.

They were supposed to love God.
They were supposed to live their life in a way that pleased God (which meant loving other people).
They were supposed to look to God for everything.

Sad to say, things didn't turn out like that.
Sometimes the Israelites did things God's way and other times they didn't.
Even with the help of a whole bunch of kings, judges (wise leaders) and prophets (people handpicked by God to tell them what God wanted them to hear) they couldn't seem to make a go of it.
Which is where Jesus comes in ...

We Wish You A Merry Christmas

Most people are pretty familiar with the Christmas story – you know, wise men, shepherds, angels, Mary and Joseph, a stable-full of animals and a bright shining star.
(If you've done a school nativity play then you'll know what I'm talking about).
What most people don't know is *why* there's a Christmas story in the first place.

So here's a bit of background info ...

For starters we all now know that stuff about our friendship with
God being broken by Adam and Eve (and if you don't then
you've probably gone and skipped the first bit of this book –
naughty, naughty!).

We've had a quick look at how disobeying God really spoiled
everything.

We've seen how God got Abram to start a new nation of people
who did things *his* way not *their* way.

And we've seen how they failed time and time again.

But what we *haven't* had checked out is what God told the
Israelites to do to keep things at least ticking over between him
and them, even during the times when they blew it.

There was one thing and one thing only that helped people to
keep people in God's good books and that was something called
'**sacrifice**'.

If your reaction to this useful
piece of information is this ...

... then I probably need to explain what I'm talking about.

Because the Israelites were God's special nation he wanted to make sure that not only was he looking out for them from heaven, but that he was also living among them.

(Okay, so that might sound impossible to you and me but living in two places at once is absolutely *no* problem for someone like God.)

All the time that the Israelites travelled around living in tents then God kept them company and lived in a very special tent of his own called the '**Tabernacle**'.

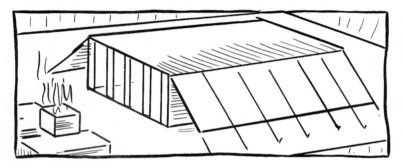

Once the Israelites had settled in Canaan the Tabernacle was replaced by the '**Temple**'.

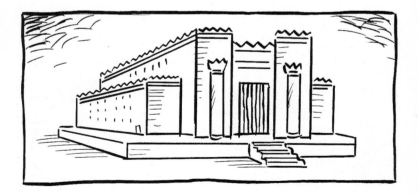

So, what exactly went on in the Tabernacle and the Temple?

Put simply, it was the place where the Israelites got the chance to meet with God.

Now that might sound a great idea until you realise who God is and what he's like.

The Bible says that God is **holy**, which means he isn't like us at all.

The Bible says that God is awesomely **powerful**, he's **pure**, he's **mighty**, he's ... well, he's **God**.

That means that if want to meet him you're going to need to be the same as him (pure, holy, perfect etc) otherwise you'll end up in serious trouble.

The Bible says that because God is so perfect and holy, nothing bad can enter his presence without being destroyed.

Which, as far as I can see, rules out the entire human race in one stroke.

But all is not lost, because God had already thought of that.

God told the Israelites that the first thing they needed to do was to employ men whose job it was to come into the Tabernacle or Temple to meet with him.

This wasn't something for any old Tom, Dick or Harry.

Meeting God was a job for the select few.
These special Israelites were called **priests**.
Just in case you're wondering what went on during these meetings, well let me tell you for nothing, it most certainly wasn't a cosy chat.
The priest's one main job was to present to God sacrifices so that all the bad stuff the Israelites had done could be forgiven.

Right from the beginning of time God made it perfectly clear that when people present an animal (or some other offering) to him he will forgive them whatever they have done wrong because it is a sign that they are really sorry.

Boring Bible Fact:
The Bible calls doing wrong 'sin'.

Getting your sins forgiven might been good news for *people* but it wasn't so appealing to the *animals*.
They had to be killed and it was their blood being shed that did the job in God's eyes.
This might sound a bit gory and a bit of a raw deal for the poor animal but later in this book you'll see why it was necessary.

The thing to remember in all this is that God wasn't being cruel and horrid. He was doing all this in preparation for restoring our friendship with him.

Anyway, hang on in there and *all* will be revealed!

One thing *no* amount of animal sacrifices could *ever* do was actually get rid of sin.
All the sacrifices did was to keep the peace between people and God until a time came when sin itself could be sorted once and for all.
That might sound like a tall order but tall orders are God's speciality.

Fascinating Rumour

There is a story that has been going round for hundreds of years that the High Priest, whose job it was to meet with God, once a year (face to face) had to have a rope tied around his ankle just in case he died while he was in God's awesome presence. The rope was to drag him out of the Holy of Holies. This might be a brilliant story but there's not much evidence to support it!

Now, where were we?

Oh yes, we'd started out talking about Christmas, hadn't we? Well, the point of all that stuff about sacrifices was that Jesus, (God's Son – for the full story get your hands on a copy of Boring Bible book *Super Son*) had made the trip from heaven to earth to be a **once-and-for-all** sacrifice for the whole human race.

Everything that had been going on, right from the beginning of time, when Adam and Eve had let God down, up until the time Jesus was born in a smelly stable in Bethlehem, was all just God setting the stage.

It's like when you go to the theatre to see a show and everything's ready for the star to make his or her big entrance.

The script has been written, the rest of the cast are in place, the scenery's been painted and the audience are in their seats waiting with eager anticipation ...

I WOULD BE IF I COULD SEE THE STAGE!

In short, Jesus was born, grew up and then set about telling people that at last they had the chance to patch things up with God.

(The Bible can tell you about this in a bit more detail; in fact there are four different accounts of Jesus's life to choose from so take your pick from Matthew, Mark, Luke and John.)

ADVANCE WARNING: THIS NEXT SECTION IS REALLY TITCHY!

Mission Accomplished!

On the very same day that the Israelites were busily getting ready to bring to God their annual animal sacrifices, Jesus allowed himself to be executed by the authorities.

Being both God and a man at the same time he'd never once sinned.

Jesus was killed, his blood flowed out of his body and as far as God was concerned (at long last) here was a perfect sacrifice that met his high standards.

One perfect person took the punishment for the sin of the world and at last the way was open for people to become friends with God again.

Power Shower

If something brilliant has happened, like your favourite soccer team winning or your favourite band getting to number one, then what's the betting you'll want to tell the world about it? Jesus knew that the whole world needed to hear that they could be friends with the God who'd made them, so he'd already organised a tip-top sales force before he died.

They were called his disciples and their job was to carry on doing the sort of things that Jesus had been doing while he was on earth.

SUCH AS...?

Such as ... healing the sick.

Such as ... raising the dead.

Such as ... telling people how God wanted them to live.

Such as ... loving people.

Such as ... telling them how they can get God's forgiveness.

There was just one *extremely* important detail that I omitted to tell you about Jesus and it's *this* ...

Three days after he'd died Jesus came out of the tomb (in which he'd been laid) to prove to everyone that God's brilliant plan to get rid of sin had worked.

In fact, over **500** hundred people saw Jesus in different places and at different times.

But Jesus wasn't planning to hang around.

He was headed back to heaven – **mission accomplished!**

Just before he returned Jesus promised his disciples that once he was back home in heaven with God (his Father) he'd send them all the power that they would ever need do everything that *he'd* been doing.

This power was called the **Holy Spirit** and when he showed up (which he did, big time, and which you can read about in Boring Bible book *Hyper Holy Happenings*) the disciples' lives were changed for ever.

With the Holy Spirit living inside of them they set about telling the world all about Jesus and showing by the miracles they performed that what they were saying was true.

And *that* was how the church began – but to find out more about that you'll need to read Boring Bible book *Saints Alive!*

Over To You!

So, you see, *that's* why you need to become a Christian.

You need to get back to becoming best friends with the God who made you.

Still not convinced?

Then what's called for is a good old spot of investigating to help you make up your mind.

Let's uncover the lowdown of some the world's most famous Christians so that we can discover what exactly it was that made them tick.

And who better to carry out the undercover work than our very own Boring Bible investigator from Boring Bible book *Hyper Holy Happenings*.

Yes, zat, I mean, that *is* you we are referring to, Inspector.

Oh, fine thanks.
How about you?

I think that's enough of the pleasantries.
We've got some investigating to do, or rather, *you* have.
On with the detective work, Inspector, before the readers
demand a refund ...

Name: Corrie Ten Boom
Born: 1892
Place of birth: Holland
Important info: Grew up in a Christian household. Taught by parents to rely upon God. Corrie had to put this into practice in the second world war when she was captured by the Nazi (German) enemy after secretly helping Jewish people to escape from them.

The German army made life extremely hard, particularly for the Jews, but Corrie and her family loved the Jews. The Bible says the Jews are God's special nation. In fact *Jesus* was a Jew and most of the Bible has come to us *through* the Jews.
Corrie got involved in what was called the 'underground'. These were Dutch people who worked against the Nazis in secret.

As the war continued, more and more Jewish people needed help to avoid being captured by the Germans and taken to their terrible prison camps.

Corrie's bedroom was fitted with a false wall for the Jews to hide in until one fateful day when they were betrayed into the hands of the enemy.

What happened next:
Corrie and her sister Betsie ended up in one of these prison camps and endured awful conditions.

Life was cheap and many people were killed or died of sickness.

All through this terrible ordeal both Corrie and her sister didn't stop trusting in God. Many times they prayed to God for strength or protection and each time God came to their rescue.

Not only did they share God's love and the good news about Jesus with the fellow inmates, but sometimes also with their German captors.

Even after Corrie had been cruelly whipped by a guard for not working hard enough, Corrie prayed for the guards.

Despite so much misery Corrie *never* gave in to hatred.
Jesus said Christians had to love their enemies and Corrie did
just that!

Betsie died in the prison camp after falling ill but Corrie was
miraculously released just one week before all the women her
age in the camp were killed.

There'd been a mix up and she should never have been set free.
Corrie knew that this was God's doing so she could tell her story
to the world.

She did just that until the day she died at the age of 91.

EET IS OBVIOUS THAT THIS REMARKABLE
LADY DIDN'T JUST TALK ABOUT BEING A
CHRISTIAN –SHE LIVED IT OUT AS WELL!
SO, MY FIRST EENVESTIGATION REVEALS
ZAT BEING A CHRISTIAN MEANS YOU 'AVE
GOT TO, 'OW YOU SAY, GET STUCK IN!
NOW, WHO EES NEXT?
AH YES! NATE SAINT. LET ME TAKE A
CLOSER LOOK AT THIS MAN'S STORY AND
SEE WHAT I CAN DEESCOVER...

Name: Nate Saint
Born: 1923
Place of birth: USA
Important info: Went as a missionary (with three other missionaries and their families) to tell the Indians of Ecuador (the Quechas, Jivaros etc) in South America about Jesus.

Nate was a pilot so he flew around dropping off supplies to other missionaries and taking people from place to place in that isolated region. Nate and his fellow missionaries felt that God was telling them to go one step further and make contact with the Huaorani tribe of Indians. This was a big risk, because these were a savage people who had little or no contact with the outside world and would kill a stranger on sight. Their neighbours called them the Aucas, which means 'savages' in Quechua.

The plan was to build up a friendship with the Huaorani tribe by dropping down gifts from the air.

With time, more and more Huaorani ventured out to receive Nate's gifts.

After three months, Nate and his colleagues sensed that the time was right to make ground contact. The group flew in and set up camp. The missionaries were armed with guns but were resolved not to use them even if it meant being killed themselves. The guns would be a last resort and would only be used to warn off attackers.

It was a Friday and a man, a woman and a teenage girl from the Huaorani tribe ventured out to meet them. This friendly first meeting lasted for a few hours. On Saturday no one showed up. On Sunday afternoon, 8 January 1956 at about three in the afternoon all five missionaries were speared to death at their camp with no apparent signs of a struggle.

What happened next:

When news got out that Nate Saint and his friends had lost their lives attempting to tell the Huaorani about Jesus the result was *amazing*. 20 US pilots immediately volunteered to take Nate's place.

More than 1,000 college students volunteered to become foreign missionaries because of this story. The number of Indians going to church shot through the roof and so did the number becoming Christians.

In fact, within a short space of time the Huaorani Indians realised that they'd made a big mistake killing the missionaries and they also became followers of Jesus.

SUCH A SAD STORY BUT SUCH A HAPPY ENDING. MY EENVESTIGATIVE POWERS TELL ME ZAT BEING A CHRISTIAN IS COSTLY. EET IS CERTAINLY NOT FOR ZEE, 'OW YOU SAY, COWARDY CUSTARDS, NON? WE MUST MOVE SWIFTLY ON. I 'AVE ZEE FILE OF GLADYS AYLWARD NOW TO LOOK INTO...

Name: Gladys Aylward
Born: 1903
Place of birth: London
Important info: She gave her life to God (another way of saying she became a Christian) at a 'revival' meeting and very soon became convinced that God was calling her to preach the Gospel (another way of saying 'the good news about Jesus') in China. At the age of 26, with absolutely no qualifications and not even enough money to travel by ship, she set out for China.

Her long journey took her through Russia and Japan, by train, bus, boat and mule. Young Gladys eventually arrived at the mountainous Shansi province and headed for the city of Yangchen, where she met up with Jeannie Lawson, an elderly missionary who'd been there for years.

Yangchen was a stopping place for the mule caravans which travelled across that inhospitable terrain, so Gladys and Jeannie made the place in which they lived into an inn.

Travellers were put up for the night and their mules fed and watered but they got more than they bargained for. The two ladies kept the travellers entertained during the long evenings with tales about a man named Jesus.

As time went by, many of these men became Christians themselves and the inn became a popular stopping off point.

What happened next:

After the death of Jeannie Lawson, Gladys was introduced to the Mandarin (a high ranking official) of Yangchen. He employed Gladys as a government inspector to make sure upper and middle class ladies had their feet bound properly. (According to custom small feet were considered to be graceful, so girls had their feet wrapped tightly in bandages to keep them tiny.) Gladys saw this as an opportunity to meet these ladies and tell them about Jesus.

Glady Aylward became well-respected because of her care for prisoners and the poor. She even got the nickname '**Ai-weh-deh**' which means '**virtuous one**'.

But things soon changed for Gladys ...

She came across a child begging by the side of the road.
The young girl was in a very poor state and the woman she was
with was very obviously not her mother and had kidnapped the
girl to help her beg. Gladys 'bought' the little girl off the woman
for ninepence so she could care for the unfortunate child.

'Ninepence' (as the girl was known) soon became one child
among *many* as Gladys took in more and more orphans.
With the coming of the second world war China was attacked by
the Japanese.

Gladys managed to lead nearly
100 orphans over the treacherous
mountains to safety.
Due to ill health, Gladys Aylward
eventually returned to England but
she *never* stopped telling people
about Jesus.

Name: Paul (originally called Saul).
Born: Date not known
Place of birth: Tarsus in Cilicia
Important info: Paul was a Jew who was brought up to do everything a Jew was required to by Jewish law and tradition. As he grew into manhood Paul was determined to be the *best* Jew on the block. You couldn't fault him.

When the first Christian (Stephen) was stoned to death for being a follower of Jesus, Paul was on hand to hold the cloaks of the 'stoners'.

Not content with that, Paul set about persecuting the Christians, hunting them down, getting them thrown into jail or worse still; **executed**. He'd stop at *nothing* to hound down these people he felt were against everything his religion stood for.

And then, one day, while heading for a town called Damascus in pursuit of more Christians, he was stopped in his tracks by Jesus himself, in all his brilliance.

Paul was blinded by Jesus's brightness. Jesus told Paul that from now on he would be working for *him*. Such was the impact of Paul's encounter with Jesus that his life changed from that moment on.

What happened next:
From then on Paul put as much energy into telling people about Jesus as he'd put in the past into trying to wipe Christians from the face of the earth.
He travelled all across the Roman world telling Jews and Gentiles (that's everyone who isn't a Jew) that Jesus really *is* the Son of God and he's alive.

(He should know – he'd met him face to face).
Paul suffered just about every sort of hardship imaginable.

He was flogged, beaten, stoned, imprisoned, shipwrecked, attacked, hungry, thirsty, abused and ridiculed.
None of this deterred Paul from making sure as many people as

possible knew that they too could get back into God's family, the job Jesus had personally commanded him to do.
Paul set up churches all over the place, and when he wasn't on hand to encourage the church members face to face he was busy writing letters to them.
The New Testament bit of the Bible features quite a lot of Paul's letters, and here are some snippets from a few of them ...

Now that we have been put right with God through faith, we have peace with God through our Lord Jesus Christ.

That was taken from one of Paul's letters to the church in Rome. You can find it in the Bible in the book called Romans and in chapter 5 and verse 1.

Here's a letter Paul wrote to the Christians in a place called Ephesus ...

From Paul, who by Christ's will is an apostle of Christ Jesus –

To God's people in Ephesus, who are faithful in their life in union with Christ Jesus: May God our Father and the Lord Jesus Christ give you grace and peace.

Let us give thanks to the God and Father of our Lord Jesus Christ! For in our union with Christ he has blessed us by giving us every spiritual blessing in the heavenly world.

*Even before the world was made, God had already chosen us to be his through our union with Christ,
so that we would be holy and without fault before him.*

You can find *that* one in the Bible book Ephesians in chapter 1 and from verse 1 through to verse 4.
And last but not least one more snippet from Paul's prolific pen ...

May you always be joyful in your union with the Lord. I say it again: Rejoice!

Show a gentle attitude towards everyone.
The Lord is coming soon.

Don't worry about anything, but in all your prayers ask God for what you need, always asking him with a thankful heart.

And God's peace, which is far beyond human understanding will keep your hearts and minds safe in union with Christ Jesus.

You'll find that one in the book of Philippians chapter 4 and from verses 4 to 7.

Paul worked miracle after miracle by the power God had given him and countless people were healed of sicknesses as a result. Not only did Paul tell ordinary folk about Jesus, he also had the chance to come before rulers and officials to tell his story.

His top public appearance was when he stood before Caesar (the Roman emperor) in Rome itself.

It was shortly after this that Paul died (probably executed for being a Christian).

Thanks, Inspector.

> MA PLEASURE, MONSIEUR! PLEASE DON'T 'ESITATE TO CALL ME IN ZEE FUTURE EEF YOU NEED A SPOT OF, 'OW YOU SAY, UNDERCOVER WORK DOING. AU REVOIR!

Okay, so we've had quite a lot of information to absorb, so what I suggest is we press the '**Fast Rewind Button**' ...

... and have a speedy recap of the main bits, just in case there's anything you've forgotten.

How does that sound?

(Not that I'd expect for *one moment* that anything's slipped your mind – intelligent readers that you are!)

Right, let's **go**!

So, that's where we've got to so far.

Now it's up to **you**.

In a minute I'm going to give you your very own chance to follow in the footsteps of the courageous people you've being reading about.

Being a Christian is a **serious business** but it's not something anyone can do *for* you.

It's something that's *personal*.

Just between **you** and **God**.

But first, it's really, *really* important that you know what you're letting yourself in for.

When you buy something from a shop like a camera or CD player or a mobile phone I'll bet you spend *ages* flicking throught the catalogues until you've found just the right one.

You carefully read up all the info to see whether it does what you want it to do.

I WASN'T EXPECTING MY MINI-DISC PLAYER TO BE QUITE SO MINI!

If your mobile phone only does great ringtones and plays cool games but *can't* make calls then it's not gonna be much use as a phone, is it?

Before you buy into being a Christian (however brill or cool that may sound) let's check through what you're going to get for your money. (Okay, so it's free and won't cost you a penny but you know what I'm getting at!).

**WANT TO MAKE
THE MOST OF YOUR LIFE?**

WANT TO MAKE NEW FRIENDS?
(e.g. God)

**WANT TO FIND OUT THE REASON
YOU'RE ALIVE?**

Then you need new...

CHRISTIANITY™

**OFFER ONLY VALID
WHILE YOU'RE
ALIVE,**
LIMITED TO
ONE PER PERSON

Becoming a Christian is as simple as ... well it's as simple as ... **BECOMING A CHRISTIAN!**
For a once and once only payment
(full details further on) all of these **amazing** goodies are **yours**!

FORGIVENESS OF YOUR SIN

A BRILL FRIENDSHIP WITH GOD

THE HOLY SPIRIT TO COME AND LIVE INSIDE OF YOU

A NEW HEART (NO, NOT A HEART WITH BLOOD) BUT A HEART THAT CARES AND WANTS TO PLEASE GOD

A PRE-BOOKED PLACE IN HEAVEN WHEN YOU DIE

Plus much, much more besides!
THIS IS A ONCE-IN-A-LIFETIME
(your lifetime, actually)
OPPORTUNITY AND MOST
DEFINITELY *NOT* **TO BE MISSED!**

There isn't one, but we should warn you that changing your mind at a later date is not advisable. We therefore recommend that every care is taken *before* purchase to ensure **maximum** future satisfaction.

METHOD OF PAYMENT

No credit cards of other forms of payment are acceptable. Friendship with God can only be paid for with your life. Simply hand over your life to Jesus and make him **No.1** and *he'll* do the rest.

WARNING: Please note that **CHRISTIANITYTM** must be handled with caution.

CHRISTIANITYTM comes complete with built-in **FWG** (**F**riendship **W**ith **G**od) which must be cared for and maintained according to your instruction manual (Bible). To guarantee maximum fulfillment from **CHRISTIANITYTM** regular communication (prayer) with the manufacturer (God) is essential.

CHRISTIANITYTM comes with an extended warranty. (It's extended forever!)

NO REFUNDS AVAILABLE

FOR BEST RESULTS KEEP IN FULL PUBLIC VIEW.

AVOID STORING AWAY SOMEWHERE OUT OF SIGHT AS THE PRODUCT TENDS TO DETERIORATE.

AND WHATEVER YOU DO DON'T FORGET TO TELL YOUR FRIENDS THAT YOU'VE SIGNED UP TO **CHRISTIANITY**TM

Delivery of your **CHRISTIANITY**TM is instant so there's absolutely **no waiting** involved (or for that matter, any postage costs).

So don't delay – sign up today!

YOU KNOW IT MAKES SENSE!

Hmm, looks like an offer you can't refuse, doesn't it?
But are you ready to make Jesus **No.1** in your life?
That's quite a hard question isn't it?
Still not sure?
Well, check out these cartoons and see if you can work out by the end what letting Jesus be **No.1** in your life means.

Jesus ISN'T No.1...

Jesus IS No.1...

Jesus ISN'T No.1...

Jesus IS No.1...

Jesus ISN'T No.1...

Jesus IS No.1...

Jesus ISN'T No.1...

Jesus IS No.1...

Becoming a Christian is the best thing you can ever do, but it's also the *hardest* because it means you've gotta turn your back on doing things the way *you* want to do them and do things *God's* way.

But don't worry, God's not a spoilsport.

He's the one who made everything so he should know how to have a good time.

In fact the Bible says that God wants the absolute **best** for your life.

Here's what Jesus said ...

MY PURPOSE IS TO GIVE YOU LIFE AND GIVE IT TO THE FULL.

Now get your thinking brains on (that's if you haven't got them on already) and make a **Top Ten** list of anything you can think of that you reckon spoils the world.

Let me help get you started.

How about ... '**People fighting**'.

My Top Ten List
of things that spoil the world

1 _____

2 _____

3 _____

4 _____

5 _____

6 _____

7 _____

8 _____

9 _____

10 _____

Now I won't pretend that I know what you've written, but I'm guessing that you haven't had *too much* trouble thinking up ten ideas.

But before you get too depressed thinking about what you've just written I'm now going to give you a **Top Ten** list of some of the things that **Jesus** can give us to make things better.

Here goes ...

My Top Ten List
of things that Jesus did to make the world better.

1 Gets rid of our sin _____

2 Forgives us _____

3 Heals our sicknesses _____

4 Gives us joy _____

5 Gives us peace _____

6 Gives us a reason for our lives _____

7 Helps us love each other _____

8 Provides us with food and clothes and homes _____

9 Comforts us when we're upset _____

10 Protects us _____

The Bible says that with God living inside us (that's the Holy Spirit) the world can be made a better place, which is exciting isn't it?

And if you become a Christian that means God's going to use you (yes, **you**) to brighten up the world right where you live. (Or maybe even some other country when you're older.)

So, being a Christian isn't just about going to church – it's about being an **Agent of God**, doing God's work, with the power that God gives you.

If you're up for it then let's do something about it.

But hold your horses!

I think I ought to give you a bit more thinking time so let's whiz back in time to the year **AD64** and find out what life was like for those *early* Christians.

No, not *that* sort of early Christian.
This sort ...

ROME ECHO

AD 64 SUMMER SPECIAL

ROME BURNS

Following the terrible fire that has destroyed almost three quarters of the city over a period of six days and seven nights Emperor Nero has been accused of starting the blaze for his own amusement. In an attempt to deflect these criticisms Nero has laid the blame squarely at the feet of the city's Christian population.

Our on the spot reporter, Tacitus, brings the following report.

"Therefore, to stop the rumour (that he had set Rome on fire), he (Emperor Nero) falsely charged with guilt, and punished with the most fearful tortures, the persons commonly called Christians, who were hated for their enormities. Christus, the founder of that name, was put to death as a criminal by Pontius Pilate, procurator of Judea, in the reign of Tiberius ... Those who were arrested who confessed they were Christians were convicted not so much on the charge of burning the city as "hating the human race".

In their very deaths they were made subjects of sport for they were covered with the hides of wild beasts, and worried to death by dogs, or nailed to crosses or set fire to and when the day waned, burned to serve for the evening lights.

These are all excerpts taken from a *true* account by Tacitus, a Roman historian who had lived in Rome as a young boy during

the time Christians were being tortured for what they believed. *Why* were they tortured? Probably because the Emperor felt that Jesus was a big threat to him.

After all, Jesus was **God** and Nero was just a **human** ruler. If Christians were worshipping *Jesus* then they weren't worshipping *him*.

And as far as *Nero* was concerned that just **wouldn't do**! (If you want to find out some more about mad, bad Emperor Nero and other loads of other stuff about the Romans, then check out Boring Bible book *Hyper Holy Happenings*)

Now let's get down to business ...

The Boring Bible Guide to Becoming a Christian

(in five easy-ish steps)

Step 1:

You've gotta believe that there really *is* a God who made the whole universe, the world and even you. And you've gotta believe that God loves you very, very much and that he's made you for a very special reason.

(You are not, repeat **not**, an accident).

Step 2:

You've gotta say sorry to God (from the bottom of your heart so you've really got to mean it) for all the wrong things you've done.

If you're not completely sure if something is wrong than ask God to tell you if it is. If you suddenly feel uneasy about it then you've probably done wrong.

Step 3:

You've gotta repent.

All repenting means is turning around and going in the other direction.

It means it's no good saying 'sorry' to God for doing wrong then straight away doing the same thing all over again.

That would mean that you don't really mean what you mean – if you know what I mean?!

Repenting means you've got to decide that you don't want to keep on doing wrong. You've gotta want to do things *God's* way from now on.

But never fear, you don't have to go it alone on this one. Once you become a Christian you'll have the **Holy Spirit** with you all the way to help you make the right decisions.

And whatever you do, don't start fretting when you do things wrong, because you will sometimes. Just ask God to forgive you and he'll wipe what you've done from his memory banks! What God's *really* interested in is whether you're *serious* about trying to get it right; and if you are, then *he'll* help you.

Bit by bit you'll find you're doing things God's way and not your own way any more.

Now, *that's* what I call progress!

KEEP UP THE GOOD WORK!

Step 4:

You've gotta believe that 2,000 years ago, Jesus visited Planet Earth as a baby and that his dad was actually God in heaven even though his mum, Mary, was a human. (Check out the lowdown in Boring Bible book *Super Son*).

That bit's really, *really* important!

You've also gotta believe that Jesus didn't do **one** wrong thing ('cos he was God) and that he allowed himself to be punished (by God his Father in heaven) for our sin.

(That's the bit where Jesus was executed on a wooden cross by the Romans.)

You've gotta believe that God proved that he accepted Jesus's sacrifice by bringing him back to life **three days later** and that he's now in heaven with God.

(That bit's *also* really important – in fact it's *so* important that we've dedicated a whole section to it a bit later, so keep your eyes peeled for it).

If you believe all that you've just read, then it means you believe that there doesn't have to be any horrid sin getting in the way of you and God being friends.

Step 5:

You've gotta say "**thank you**" to Jesus for taking away your sin and tell him you want *him* to be **No.1** in your life from now on. The moment you do that God has promised that he'll send his Holy Spirit to come and live right inside you, so you know deep down that you're forgiven and that you now belong to him.

Is that good or **what**?

Fascinating Fact:

Did you know that because the Holy Spirit sets up home inside of you, the Bible calls you a 'Temple' of the Holy Spirit. That's why God's got millions of homes, 'cos there are millions and millions of Christians round the world who've got God living inside them. Awesome, eh?

SORRY, YOU'VE GOT THE WRONG HOUSE! GOD LIVES NEXT DOOR.

Action Stations!

If you've understood everything we've talked about and now want to get your life right with God than you need to talk to him about it.

The chances are you might not be sure what to say, so here's a prayer (prayer means talking to God) that will lead you into an amazing friendship with God.

Read it through first just so you understand what you're gonna be saying and then, when you're ready, find a quiet place and read it out loud (or at least so you can hear what you're saying).

Here's the prayer ...

> Dear God.
>
> Thank you that you love me and
> want to be my friend.
>
> I'm really sorry for doing wrong
> things and living life my way.
>
> Please forgive me.
>
> Thank you Jesus that you love me so
> much you were willing to
> take the punishment for my sin.
>
> From now on I want to live your
> way, not my way.
>
> Thank you for the Holy Spirit to help me do that.
>
> I now hand over my life to you Jesus
> and ask you to come and live inside me.
>
> Thank you that you have accepted me into your
> family and that I'm now a child of God.
>
> Amen

CONGRATULATIONS!
If you've prayed that prayer and really meant it then you are now a **Christian**.
Why not mark this special occasion by filling in this Boring Bible commemorative certificate to remind you what you've done.

This is to certify that on the

...........Sunday.....17th....October.2004...(date)

............Rachel...Cann.........................(your name)

handed his/her life over to Jesus, lock, stock and barrel

and has now become a **Christian**

(or an **Agent of God** if you think that sounds better)

Boring Bible Fact:
Did you know that you've just started a party in heaven?

Don't worry, relax, you're not invited anyway.

Here's what the Bible says ...

The angels of God rejoice over one sinner who repents.

(Luke chapter 15 verse 10)

I suppose you could always throw yourself your own mini party right here and now.

The Bible is really big on celebrating (check it out if you don't believe me and you'll discover how many different festivals God has organised).

And one of the *best* ways of celebrating is with a good old sing-song.

The Bible's packed with songs that the Israelites used to sing to God when they wanted to have a party in his honour.

They're called the Psalms and I've picked out a few of my favourites.

(On second thoughts, you can forget about the singing bit. You don't want to upset your neighbours, now, do you?)

Just read them out loud, I think that'll do just fine.

Oh, and don't forget to get yourself some food and drink.

You can't *possibly* have a party without nosh!

Okay, so here come the psalms ...

And that's the *whole* of Psalm 100.

PRAISE GOD WITH SHOUTS OF JOY,
ALL THE PEOPLE!
SING TO THE GLORY OF HIS NAME.
OFFER HIM GLORIOUS PRAISE!
SAY TO GOD, "HOW WONDERFUL ARE
THE THINGS YOU DO!
YOUR POWER IS SO GREAT THAT
YOUR ENEMIES BOW DOWN IN FEAR
BEFORE YOU.
EVERYONE ON EARTH WORSHIPS YOU,
THEY SING PRAISES TO YOU,
THEY SING PRAISES TO
YOUR NAME."

That was out of Psalm 66 and the first four verses.
What's next?
Oh yes, Psalm 47 and verse 1 to 2 and 6 to 8.
Read on!

The next one up is Psalm 33 (or at least the first bit of it).
So, what are you waiting for?
Blast it out!

ALL YOU THAT ARE RIGHTEOUS, SHOUT FOR JOY FOR WHAT THE LORD HAS DONE. PRAISE HIM, ALL YOU THAT OBEY HIM. GIVE THANKS TO THE LORD WITH HARPS, SING TO HIM WITH STRINGED INSTRUMENTS. SING A NEW SONG TO HIM, PLAY THE HARP WITH SKILL AND SHOUT FOR JOY!

And last, but by no means least, a little burst of good old Psalm 103 ...

Okay, party time over, let's get back to business.

Can I ask you a question?

Well I'm going to anyway.
When you get some good news, what do you do with it?

That's right.
The chances are you won't want to keep it to yourself.
So, it's probably a jolly good idea if you share *your* good news about becoming a Christian with someone else.
Go and hunt down someone you know and tell them that you've just become a Christian.

Here are some of the reactions you might get ...

Or maybe ...

Or even ...

So be prepared!

But whatever happens don't worry if they're not as enthusiastic as you, it's still good to make public what a great step you've made.

All alone!

For all I know you could be the only Christian in your family or your school or your neighbourhood.

That makes following Jesus a real toughie, doesn't it?

What you need to know is that although you might *feel* all alone in the world, you're most definitely **not**.

The Boring Bible Investigation Department has been foraging around for some fascinating facts that will encourage you to see that being a Christian means you're part of something **big** ...

Did you know that it's estimated that roughly **174,000** people become Christians **every day**?

Did you know that it's estimated that approximately **3,500** new churches are started around the world **every week**?

Did you know that there are thought to be **more** Christians alive today than the total number of Christians that there have been right through history?

Did you know that **34%** of the world's population are thought to be Christians? That'a a whopping 1.95 **billion** people (give or take the odd one or two).

The Great Resurrection Riddle

A few pages back I said we were going to check out this whole thing about Jesus actually coming back to life again, three days after he'd been executed by the Romans.

To be honest, it's not the sort of thing that happens every day, so we can hardly just skip over it without checking it out properly. So, the big question is:

Why exactly did Jesus need to be raised back to life?

For starters, Jesus was God (in a human body) which means that he needed to end up back in heaven (that's where God lives) once he'd finished his mission to earth.

Being stuck in a tomb for good would have been bad news not only for Jesus but for the *entire universe*.

Another very good reason is that although Jesus was taking the punishment for all our rotten old sin by being sacrificed, God only planned this as a one-off event. Once the job was done, Jesus could resume his place in heaven with God, his Father.

Another important thing to know is that there's two places you can end up when you die.

Er, not quite what I was meaning.

What I *meant* was that there's heaven (where God lives and it's brilliant and that's where he really wants *you* to be) and there's hell where God *doesn't* live (where it's dark and horrible and it's the very *last* place God wants you to be).

Because we're all descendants of Adam and Eve (okay, so I know it was a long time ago but you're gonna have to trust me on this one) it means that we're automatically separated from God not only in our life but *also* when we die.

I'm glad you brought that up because that's where I was heading next.

Unless, of course, you've been taking a sneaky look at my script?...

Hmm?!
Anyway, what I was about to say was that when we become a Christian we get *out* of Adam's family ...

... and we get **into** Jesus's family.

That means we not only get to enjoy all the good stuff our Father in heaven (God) wants to lavish on us right *now* 'cos we're his kids, but when we die it's ... **heaven here I come!**

I JUST LOVE HAPPY ENDINGS...ESPECIALLY WHEN THEY'RE MINE!

Fascinating Fact:

The Bible talks about Jesus as being the 'second Adam' because he gave us all a second chance with God. (Check out Bible book 1 Corinthians chapter 15 and verse 47.) The first Adam blew it but Jesus didn't, which means his family is definitely the one to be in.

Have you ever played '**Follow The Leader**'?

(Okay, so maybe you don't *nowadays*, but the chances are you did when you were younger.)

Why am I asking you such a trivial question?

Because it's the reason Jesus needed to come back to life and then return to heaven.

No, don't be silly!
I wasn't meaning you to take me *literally*.
What I meant was so that *he* can lead the way and *we* can follow on behind him.
If we become a Christian then we also become a **follower** of Jesus.
And because *Jesus* has headed back off to heaven then *we* get to follow him there as well when we die.
Phew! I'm glad *that's* cleared up.

Boring Bible Fact:
Jesus didn't come back to life like some of the people you read about in the Bible who lived for a few more years then died again. Jesus had an altogether different sort of body (a sort of heaven and earth type body) so you could touch him and see him but he could walk through walls and disappear. This sort of body would never die.

Anyway, what *you* need to know is whether or not this stuff about the resurrection (Jesus been raised from the dead) has any proof, don't you?

Which is why, at no expense spared, we've laid on our very own Boring Bible court case to check out whether what the Bible says is really true.

Silence in court. Bring on the first witness ...

Bring on the second witness ...

Bring on the third witness ...

Bring on the last witness ...

CHIEF PRIEST WILL DO. ALL THAT RIDICULOUS
RESURRECTION NONSENSE IS POPPYCOCK!
WHO EVER HEARD OF ANYTHING SO DAFT?
THE MAN THEY CLAIM TO BE THE SON OF GOD
IS DEAD. THEY PROBABLY STOLE HIS BODY
TO PERPETUATE THEIR MISCHIEVOUS
RELIGION. OR MAYBE THIS JESUS DIDN'T DIE
AT ALL. PERHAPS HE WAS UNCONSCIOUS
WHEN HE WAS LAID IN THE TOMB AND THE
COLD NIGHT AIR REVIVED HIM. YES, THAT'S
PROBABLY EXACTLY WHAT HAPPENED!

So, what do we make of all this?

Every good court case has a jury, so here's your chance to be
part of the **Boring Bible Jury** and make up your own mind
based on the evidence to hand.

First off, let's have a quick think about what we've heard so far.
There's some tricky questions that are gonna need some smart
answers if we're going to get anywhere with this one.

TRICKY QUESTION NUMBER ONE:
How could Jesus have rolled the tombstone away even if
he had somehow revived himself?

The Bible says he was in a bad way even *before*
they hung him up on the cross. He'd been
whipped and beaten so badly he was hardly
recognisable. If he *had* revived, then where did he
get his strength from?

But putting that aside, the Bible says that a spear
was thrust into Jesus side while he hung on the
cross to make absolutely *certain* he was dead.

TRICKY QUESTION NUMBER TWO:
How could the disciples have rolled the stone
away?

The Bible tells us that the Romans put a full guard
on the tomb to stop this very thing. The tomb was
even sealed so that no one, but no one, could
move the stone without being found out.

And besides, the tombstones were huge and
designed to roll *downwards* into their final position.

To roll them back again meant having to push this extremely
heavy weight uphill.

TRICKY QUESTION NUMBER THREE:
Even if they had been able to steal Jesus's
body to pretend he'd come back to life, then
why were most of them prepared to be
killed later in life for believing in Jesus?

Would you die for something *you* knew was a
lie?

I wouldn't.

Some people have even suggested that the Jewish authorities stole the body to avoid the disciples getting there first and pretending that Jesus had miraculously gone back to heaven.

TRICKY QUESTION NUMBER FOUR:
If they had, then why on earth didn't they
present the body as evidence as soon as
people started spreading stories about
Jesus being raised? It would have nipped
the whole thing in the bud and made their
life *much* easier.

Added to all this, the Bible tells us that Jesus appeared to over
500 people in all and some of them he appeared to more than
once. Jesus turned up in different places and in different ways
and over a number of days.
Meeting the risen Jesus had such a powerful effect on them that
they couldn't stop telling people about him.
It's because of *them* that we're still talking about Jesus today
(just like we are now, in fact). If they *hadn't* seen Jesus then this
whole Christian thing would have fizzled out years ago.

So, it's over to you ...

The jury's verdict *is* ...

Something Fishy

Nowadays lots of people wear a 'cross' symbol around their neck as a sign that they are Christians. It represents the cross on which Jesus was crucified (which is another way of saying 'killed on a cross').

Another really popular symbol Christians use is a **fish**. It looks like this ...

... and you can see it everywhere from car bumper stickers to little lapel badges. When another Christian sees it they know the owner is a friend of God like them.

BUT WHY A FISH? I THINK AN ELEPHANT WOULD LOOK REALLY COOL ON A BADGE OR MAYBE EVEN A HEDGEHOG!

The fish symbol goes right back to the time of the first Christians.

As we saw in that story about Nero, the Christians were having a hard time of it and it was safer not to broadcast that you followed Jesus ... that's if you wanted to live.

The fish symbol was *their* way of knowing who was on their side (and, more importantly, who *wasn't!*) Sometimes it was enough to draw the fish symbol in the dusty ground with a stick to reveal that you were a Christian.

It was really quite clever because in Greek (the language spoken by most people at that time) the initials of 'Jesus Christ, God's, Son, Saviour' (which is what Christians believe about Jesus) make up the Greek word for fish – **ICHTHUS**.

W.W.J.D.?

If you want to make your mark as a Christian in your neighbourhood then check out the very *latest* Christian symbol. (Well it's been around for a while but it's new in comparison with the 'fish' symbol)

It's called **W.W.J.D.?** which means **W**hat **W**ould **J**esus **D**o? You've probably seen it already, haven't you?

The most popular way of displaying **W.W.J.D.?** is on a wristband, but you can get it on almost anything and everything.

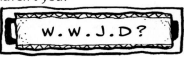

It's not only a helpful reminder, when things get tough, to see things the way *Jesus* would see them but it also helps you spot other Christians.

Fascinating Fact:

The name 'Christian' was first first used in Antioch (in Syria – there are two Antiochs in the Bible so stay alert!) around the year AD43 and was probably more of a nickname that other people called the followers of Jesus Christ rather than something they thought up themselves. It could well have even been a term of abuse. (They themselves preferred things like 'saint' or 'disciple'.) Either way it stuck, so that, as they say, was that!

So, what next?

Being a Christian doesn't mean that you can now put your feet up for the rest of your life because you're okay with God and you've got a place in heaven booked.
Nope! No way!
Being a Christian means that you've got **work** to do.

There's no catch, it's just that now you're on *God's* side he wants to use you to tell *other* people about him, like your friends or your family (that's if they don't know about Jesus already).

As I said earlier, you're now an ...

AGENT OF GOD

... and as everyone knows agents go on **missions**.
But you can't go on a mission until you've had a bit of training.
If you want to get the *full* lowdown on how to be a superb **Agent of God**, then your best bet is to buy a copy of Boring Bible book *Saints Alive!*

But being the kind and generous sort of people that we are, we've decided to at least get you up and running as a Christian.

AGENT CHECK: ONE Make sure you spend time talking to God every day. There's no point having a friend (like God) if you don't communicate.

AGENT CHECK: TWO Make sure you spend some time reading the Bible. (There's some great versions around for kids – that's presuming you don't own one already). The Bible is God's very own instruction manual so you won't know what to do unless you take time out to get stuck into it!

And while you're at it why not get hold of a copy of Boring Bible book *Bible Buster* which'll help you know *how* to read the Bible and *where* to get started.

AGENT CHECK: THREE Start going to church (that's if you don't go already). Church is the place you meet other Christians and who'll encourage and help you.

It's also the place you get taught more stuff about God so you can be more effective as one of God's agents.

At church you'll spend some time telling God how great he is by thanking him and praising him. (That's called worship and it often involves singing, so get those vocal chords tuned.)

There are plenty of different styles of Christian churches to choose from, so pick out one you feel most at home in ...

BORING BIBLE ACTIVATION STATION:
Here's your chance to put your praying into action. Why not ask God to show you the best church for to go to?

Here's a question.
Have you ever been called names at school?
(Other than your *real* name – that doesn't count).
It's not much fun, is it?

What's *much* nicer is when someone says *good* things about you.
Like ...

or ...

or even ...

Did you know ... that the Bible's full of stuff that tells us what *God* thinks about us. Yep, it really does! And when we become a Christian God's got loads more stuff he wants to say to us. Let me give you a little taster ...

What God Says About Me

(now I'm a Christian)

I'M GOD'S FRIEND

I'M FORGIVEN

I'M HOLY

I'M A SAINT (WITHOUT BEING DEAD FOR 300 YEARS!)

I'M A NEW PERSON

I'M RIGHT WITH GOD

I'M HANDPICKED BY GOD

I'M LOVED BY GOD

I'M AN HEIR OF EVERYTHING GOD HAS ('COS I'M HIS CHILD!)

I'M NOT CONDEMNED BY GOD

The Bible's jam-packed full of stuff that God wants to say to you. But being an **Agent of God** means you've gotta investigate the Bible if you wanna find it out.

Are you up for it?

Good!

Did you know ... that the Bible is also called the '**Word of God**'. And what do words do? – they **say** something.

Just to get you started, take a look at these two Bible investigations and see what God's got to say to **YOU**!

Bitesize Bible Investigations

Read this story taken from the Bible and then have a go at answering some easy questions at the end.

Zak's Tax

'Jesus went into Jericho and was passing through. There was a chief tax collector there named Zacchaeus, who was rich. He was trying to see who Jesus was, but he was a little man and could not see Jesus because of the crowd. So he ran ahead of the crowd and climbed a sycamore tree to see Jesus, who was going to pass that way. When Jesus came to that place, he looked up and said to Zacchaeus ...

HURRY DOWN ZACCHAEUS, BECAUSE I MUST STAY IN YOUR HOUSE TODAY.

Zacchaeus hurried down and welcomed him with great joy. All the people who saw it started grumbling, "This man has gone as a guest to the home of a **sinner**!"

Zacchaeus stood up and said to the Lord, "Listen, sir! I will give half my belongings to the poor, and if I have cheated anyone, I will pay him back **four times** as much."

Jesus said to him, "Salvation has come to this house today, for this man is a descendant of Abraham. The Son Man came to seek and to save the lost."

(Luke Chapter 19 verses 1 to 9)

a) Why do you think everyone hated Zacchaeus?

b) Why do think Zacchaeus wanted to see Jesus?

c) What difference did meeting Jesus make to Zacchaeus?

d) Why didn't the crowd think Jesus should have anything to do with Zacchaeus?

e) What did Jesus say about that?

Answers:

a) Because he was a tax collector (and they had a bad habit of collecting more than they should)

b) Maybe because he knew that *only Jesus could forgive him.*

c) He turned away from his bad ways.

d) Because they thought that Jesus shouldn't be interested in **bad** people.

e) Jesus said that they were *exactly the sort of people he was interested in.*

This next Bible story might be familiar to one or two of you ...

Stone me!

'The Philistines gathered for battle in Sucoh, a town in Judah. A man named Goliath from the city of Gath came out from the Philistine camp to challenge the Israelites.

He was nearly **three metres tall** and wore bronze armour that weighed about **fifty-seven kilogrammes** and a bronze helmet. Goliath stood and shouted at the Israelites, "What are you doing there, lined up for battle? Choose one of your men to fight me. If *he* wins and kills me, we will be your slaves; but if *I* win and kill him, you will be our slaves. Here and now I challenge the Israelite army. I dare you to pick someone to fight me!"

When Saul and his men heard this, they were **terrified**.

David was the son of Jesse, who was an Ephrathite from Bethlehem in Judah.

David said to Saul ...

He took his shepherd's stick and then picked up five smooth stones from the stream and put them in his bag. With his catapult ready, he went out to meet Goliath.

The Philistine started walking towards David ...

"Come on," he challenged David, "and I will give your body to the birds and animals to eat".

David answered, "You are coming against me with sword, spear, and javelin, but I come against you in the name of the Lord Almighty, **the God of the Israelite armies**, whom you have defied.

This very day the Lord will put you in my power."
Goliath started walking towards David again, and David ran
quickly towards the Philistine battle
line to fight him. He put his hand into
his bag and took out a stone, which
he slung at Goliath. It hit him on the
forehead and broke his skull, and
Goliath fell face downwards on the
ground. And so, without a sword,
David defeated and killed Goliath with
a catapult and a stone!'

(You can read the full version of this story in 1 Samuel chapter 17 verses 1 to 54.)

a) Why were Saul and the Israelite army scared?
b) Why wasn't David scared?
c) What do you think Goliath saw when David approached him?
d) How did David defeat Goliath?
e) What can you learn from this Bible story?

Answers:

a) Because they kept their eyes fixed on Goliath.
b) Because he kept his eyes fixed on **God.**
c) A weedy young lad.
d) Because he didn't trust in his own strength.
e) That when you trust in God *nothing* is impossible.

If you're a Christian then
the exciting thing is that
you can trust in God like
David did.
You don't need to be
afraid of *anything* God's
enemy throws at you.

That's because it's far more important to spend our time concentrating on *Jesus*.
But for just the record here's what you need to know.

God's Enemy

God's enemy is called Satan or the Devil and he is one of God's created beings, so he's most definitely *not* equal with God or anything like that.

He started out in heaven but decided he wanted the **No.1** slot (which belongs to God) so God threw him out of heaven (along with loads of other angels or beings, who'd also rebelled). They ended up on and around planet earth where they set up shop. The Devil was the one who tricked Adam and Eve into allowing him to be top dog on earth and from then to now, he and his underdogs have gone

around doing their level best to spoil everything that's got God's name on it (which is the whole of creation including you and me).

When Jesus died on the cross he put the Devil out of business, but the Devil's not going to leave the scene until he *has* to.

Fascinating Fact:

Jesus's very last words before he died were "It is finished!" That didn't mean that Jesus had given up. In fact, nothing could be further from the truth. What Jesus meant was that his mission to defeat the Devil had been accomplished.

Although it's just a matter of time before God's enemy is got rid of for good he still has a grudge against God, and for that matter a*nyone* who joins forces with God.
(That's us Christians I'm talking about now).
So, he's your enemy as well – but the good news is you don't have to fear him.

YOU COULD HAVE TOLD ME THAT STRAIGHT AWAY! I WAS BEGINNING TO GET A SERIOUS ATTACK OF THE COLLYWOBBLES!

All you've gotta do is stick to your guns, stick close to God and he can't touch you.

Listen to what the Bible says ...

'Submit yourselves to God, resist the Devil and he will flee from you'
James chapter 4 verse 7

What that means is if you keep Jesus as **No.1** in your lives and live your life to please God then you can stand up to the enemy like this ...

Believe it and he'll **beat it**!
In fact the Bible says a lot about not worrying about the enemy, which makes me think that the very last thing God wants you and me to be is afraid.
Remember David and how he defeated Goliath?
Well, that's how *we've* gotta be.
(Not with slingshots, obviously!)
Are you with me?
Excellent.

Promises, Promises

Most people aren't very good at keeping promises even if they really want to.

Sometimes we make a promise we have no intention of breaking, but something happens that we hadn't bargained for and we end up letting someone down.

For instance, suppose you arrange to meet your friends at the park on Saturday morning but just as you're about to go out the door …

Fortunately for us, God never, *ever* breaks a promise.
The Bible says that not only does God *not* lie but more brilliantly
... he *can't*!
Which is **good news** for us.

So, what sort of promises does God make?

Have a look some of the ones we've picked out specially for
you.
(Aren't we thoughtful?)

God's Promises

'For God has said, "I will never leave you; I will never abandon you."'
(Hebrews chapter 13 verse 5.)

'I have always loved you, so I will continue to show you my constant love.'
(Jeremiah chapter 31 verse 3.)

'Bad as you as you are, you know how to give good things to your children. How much more, then, will your Father in heaven give good things to those who ask him!'
(Matthew chapter 7 verse 11.)

'He(God) will cover you with his wings; you will be safe in his care; his faithfulness will protect and defend you.'
(Psalm chapter 91 verse 4.)

They're great promises aren't they?
The Bible's packed full of God's promises so, if you fancy a bit of investigating when you've got five minutes to spare then you know what to search for, don't you?

Well, that's just about it for this Boring Bible book.
Don't forget that there are loads more titles in the series to get your teeth into (not literally of course).

So, as you can see, you don't have to be *crazy* to be a Christian, but you do have to be *mad* about God.
Why do people think Christians are crazy?
Well, that's easy.
Most people think that being **No.1** is the best.
They think that handing over your life to God is just about the *craziest* thing you can ever do and that you're doomed to a life of dullness and utter boringness (if there is such a word, and if there *isn't*, then I've just made one up!).
But I hope that as we've looked into what being a Christian *really* is you'll have come to the conclusion that *not* letting Jesus be **No.1** in your life is probably the *craziest* thing you can ever do (or *not* do).

If you're now a Christian, or have been one for a while, don't give up when things seem a bit tough.
Keep at it!

That's what being an **Agent of God** is all about.

Boring Bible Fact:
The Bible says that Christians who don't change their mind
about following Jesus, whatever they have to put up with,
will get given a white stone when they get to heaven. On
the white stone will be written a secret codename which
only they will know.
If you don't believe me then check it out in a Bible.
Revelation chapter 2 verse 17.

Being the helpful sort of people that we are at the Boring Bible
Production HQ (my desk) we thought you'd appreciate a few
dates to put in your diary.
(I've left out my birthday 'cos I don't want everyone finding out
how old I am – only Noah and his wife are privy to that info!)

Anyway ...

Some important events on the Christian calendar that are worth knowing about ...

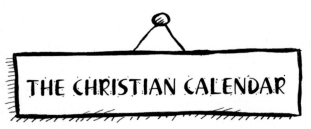

THE CHRISTIAN CALENDAR

Good Friday is when Christians remember Jesus's death. It always falls at the time of the full moon between March and April.

Easter Sunday is when Christians celebrate the resurrection of Jesus (and eat loads of chocolate!).

Ascension Day is when Christians remember Jesus's return to heaven. (40 days after Easter.)

Pentecost is when Christians celebrate God sending the Holy Spirit. (50 days after Jesus's resurrection.)

Advent is when Christians nowadays prepare for celebrating the birth of Jesus. (From December 1st through to December 24th.)

Christmas is when Christians celebrate the birth of Jesus (and give each other gifts like the wise men brought gifts to Jesus).

Fascinating Fact:

Since the time of the full moon is always changing (because the planets move around in space) Easter is never at the same date each year.
In 1703 it was on the 8th April (no I wasn't alive at the time, someone cleverer than me worked it out if you really must know).
And in the year 2266 it's going to be on 25th March (but I wouldn't rush out to by any Easter cards, you won't be around to send them).

Hope those bits of Christian trivia were helpful, and if you really *must* know, I'll now tell you when I was born.

I was born on ... oh dear, it looks like we've gone and run out of space on this page. Never mind, you'll just have to make an educated guess (but make sure it's a flattering one, okay?)

Bitesize Bible Bitz to Memorize

It's really handy to have a few bits from the Bible stored in your head so you can remind yourself about God when you can't lay your hands on a Bible.

As we've already said, the Bible is jam-packed full of stuff that God wants us to know and the best way of finding that out is by delving into the Bible yourself to see what God has to say.

If you're not sure where to start then get your **Agent of God** hands on a copy of the fantastic (okay, so I'm biased) Boring Bible book *Bible Buster*.

I meant for you to get your *own* copy, actually!

But just to get you started, we've laid on our own little spread of bits from the Bible to memorise.

So what are you waiting for.

Get stuck in!

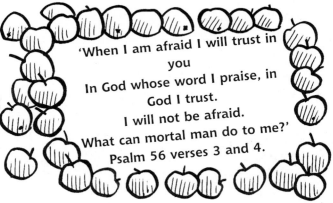

'When I am afraid I will trust in you
In God whose word I praise, in God I trust.
I will not be afraid.
What can mortal man do to me?'
Psalm 56 verses 3 and 4.

'I am the way, the truth and the life.
No one goes to the Father except by me.'
John chapter 14 verse 6.

'Trust in the Lord with all your heart.
Never rely on what you think you know.
Remember the Lord in everything you do
and he will show you the right way'.
Proverbs chapter 3 verses 5 and 6.

'If God is for us, who can be against us?'
Romans chapter 8 verse 31.

'In the beginning God created the heavens and the earth.'
Genesis chapter 1 verse 1.

'Love the Lord with all your heart, with all your soul and with all your mind. This is the greatest and the most important commandment.'
Matthew chapter 22 verses 37 and 38.

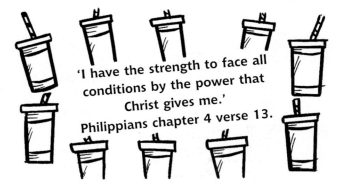

'I have the strength to face all conditions by the power that Christ gives me.'
Philippians chapter 4 verse 13.

'My God will supply all your needs out of his glorious riches in Christ Jesus.'
Philippians chapter 4 verse 19.

IF YOU'RE STILL A LITTLE BIT PECKISH THEN CHECK OUT A REAL BIBLE AND TUCK INTO LOADS MORE SCRUMMY BIBLE BITS. BON APPETIT!

Well, that's just about it for this Boring Bible book.
Don't forget, there's a whole range of other books in the series for you to enjoy, so why not collect them all?

If you're *still* not sure about this whole Christian thing and you *still* think it's all a bit **crazy** then read over some of the stuff in this book again and ask God (by praying to him) to show you if it really is for *real*.

Until the next book – **see ya**!